# EASY JAZZ FAVORITES

## *15 Selections For Young Jazz Ensembles*

## Contents

| Title | Arranger | Page |
|---|---|---|
| Ain't Misbehavin' | Lowden | 2 |
| All The Things You Are | Sweeney | 4 |
| Blue Train (Blue Trane) | Sweeney | 6 |
| Caravan | Sweeney | 8 |
| Chameleon | Sweeney | 10 |
| Fly Me To The Moon (In Other Words) | Nowak | 12 |
| The Girl From Ipanema | Berry | 14 |
| In The Mood | Sweeney | 16 |
| Inside Out | Sweeney | 18 |
| Milestones | Blair | 20 |
| A Nightingale Sang In Berkeley Square | Holmes | 22 |
| One Note Samba | Nowak | 24 |
| Route 66 | Sweeney | 26 |
| St. Louis Blues | Sweeney | 28 |
| When I Fall In Love | Holmes | 30 |

**HAL•LEONARD®**
CORPORATION

7777 W. BLUEMOUND RD. P.O. BOX 13819 MILWAUKEE, WI 53213

# AIN'T MISBEHAVIN'

Words by ANDY RAZAF
Music by THOMAS WALLER and HARRY BROOKS
Arranged by BOB LOWDEN

Guitar

# ALL THE THINGS YOU ARE
## (From VERY WARM FOR MAY)

Lyrics by OSCAR HAMMERSTEIN II
Music by JEROME KERN
Arranged by MICHAEL SWEENEY

GUITAR

**GUITAR**

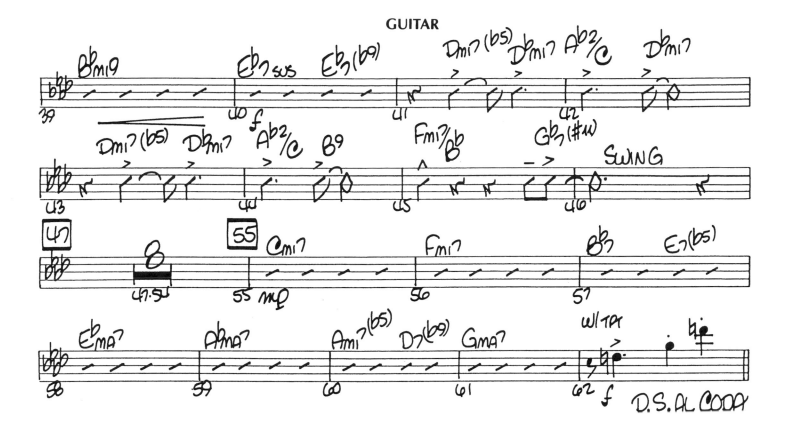

# BLUE TRAIN
## (Blue Trane)

By JOHN COLTRANE
Arranged by MICHAEL SWEENEY

GUITAR

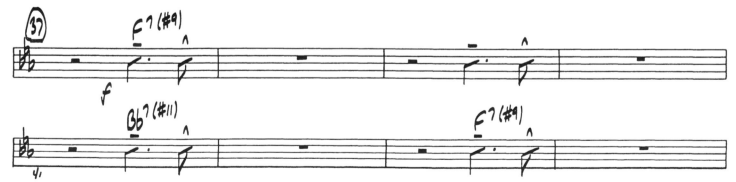

# CARAVAN
### (From SOPHISTICATED LADIES)

Words and Music by DUKE ELLINGTON,
IRVING MILLS and JUAN TIZOL
Arranged by MICHAEL SWEENEY

GUITAR

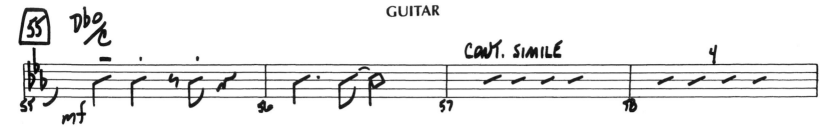

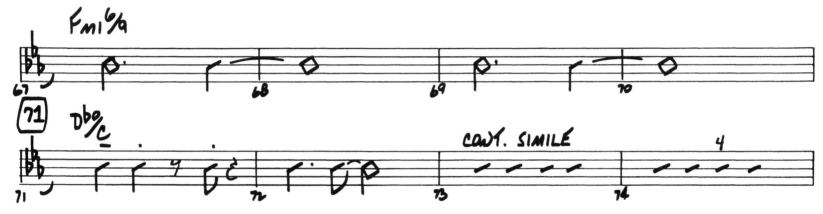

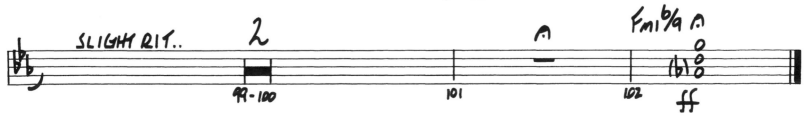

# CHAMELEON

GUITAR

By HERBIE HANCOCK, PAUL JACKSON,
HARVEY MASON and BENNIE MAUPIN
*Arranged by MICHAEL SWEENEY*

# FLY ME TO THE MOON
## (In Other Words)

Words and Music by BART HOWARD
Arranged by JERRY NOWAK

GUITAR

MODERATE SWING

EbMA9 — Fmi7/Eb — EbMA9 — Dmi7(b5) G7(b9)

*mp* — CRESC. — sim. — *mf*

**5** Cmi7 — Fmi7 — Bb7 — Bb7(b9) EbMA7

sim.

AbMA7 Ab6 AbMA7 Dmi7(b5) — G7(b9) G7 — Cmi7 — C7(b9)

**13** Fmi7 — Bb7 Fmi7 Bb7(b9) EbMA9 — Cmi7

sim.

Fmi7 — Fmi7/Bb — Bb+9 Abmi6/Eb EbMA9 — Dmi7(b5) G7(b9)

**21** Cmi7 — Fmi7 — Bb9 — Bb7(b9) EbMA7

*f* — sim.

AbMA7 Ab6 AbMA7 Dmi7(b5) — G7(b9) G7 G7(b9) Cmi7 — C7(b9)

*mf*

**29** Fmi7 — Bb9 Fmi7 Bb7/Ab Cmi7(b5) — C7 — Gb7

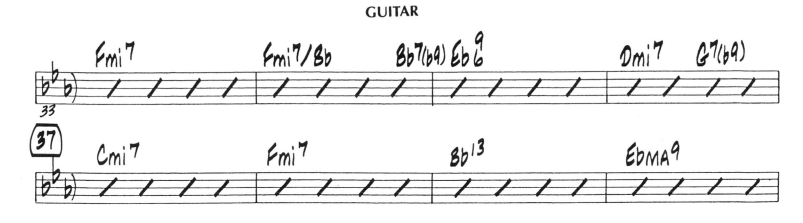

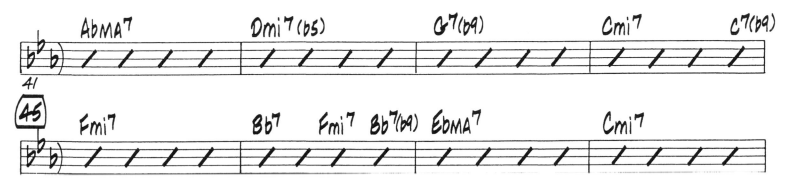

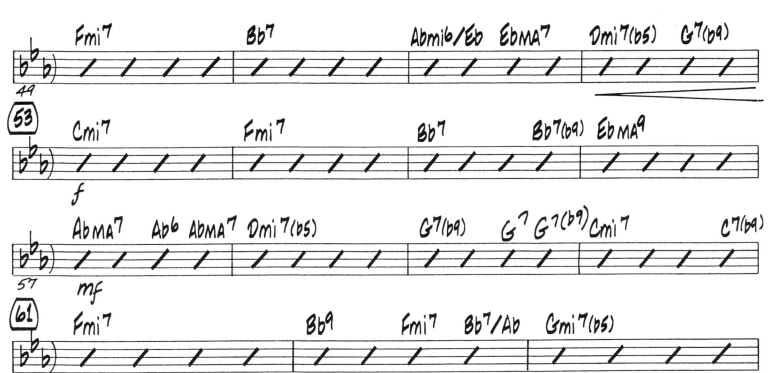

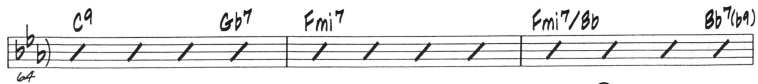

# THE GIRL FROM IPANEMA
## (Garôta De Ipanema)

Original Words by VINICIUS DE MORAES
Music by ANTONIO CARLOS JOBIM
Arranged by JOHN BERRY

GUITAR

# IN THE MOOD

By JOE GARLAND
Arranged by MICHAEL SWEENEY

Guitar

# INSIDE OUT

GUITAR

By MICHAEL SWEENEY

# MILESTONES

By **MILES DAVIS**
*Arranged by PETER BLAIR*

GUITAR

# A NIGHTINGALE SANG IN BERKELEY SQUARE

Lyric by ERIC MASCHWITZ
Music by MANNING SHERWIN
*Arranged by ROGER HOLMES*

Guitar

GMA9 EMI7 AMI11 B/D BMI7 E°7 FMI7 FMI7/Bb Bb+9
33
EbMA7 CMI7 GMI7 Eb7 A7(b5) AbMA7 G7(b9) CMI CMI7 AbMI6
GMI7 AbMA7 B13 9 BbMI7 Eb7 AbMI9 Db9 Eb6/Bb GbMI6/Bb
FMI7/Bb Bb7(b9) AbMI7 Db9 B°7 BbMI7 Eb7 AMI7 Ab13(#11)
43
GMA9 EMI7 AMI9 CMA7/D D7(b9) BMI7 Bb° Bb°7 AMI11 AMI7/D D+9
GMA7 EMI7 AMI9 CMA7/D D7(b9) BMI7 E°7 FMI7 FMI7/Bb Bb7(b9)
51
EbMA7 CMI7 GMI7 BbMI7 Eb13 9 A9(b5) AbMA7 Bb/Ab
CMI AbMI6 GMI7 FMI7 Eb7 A9(b5) AbMI9 Db9 EbMA7 FMI7 GMI7 AbMA7 GMI7
FMI7 FMI7/Bb Bb7(b9) Eb6 CMI7 FMI7 GMI7 C7(b9)
AbMI6 FMI7/Bb Bb7(b9) Db9 EMA7(b5) Eb6 9
GRAD. DECRESC.
RITARD
mp

# ONE NOTE SAMBA
## (Samba De Uma Nota So)

Original Lyrics by NEWTON MENDONCA
English Lyrics by ANTONIO CARLOS JOBIM
Music by ANTONIO CARLOS JOBIM
Arranged by JERRY NOWAK

**Guitar**

MCA music publishing

# ROUTE 66

GUITAR

By BOBBY TROUP
Arranged by MICHAEL SWEENEY

GUITAR

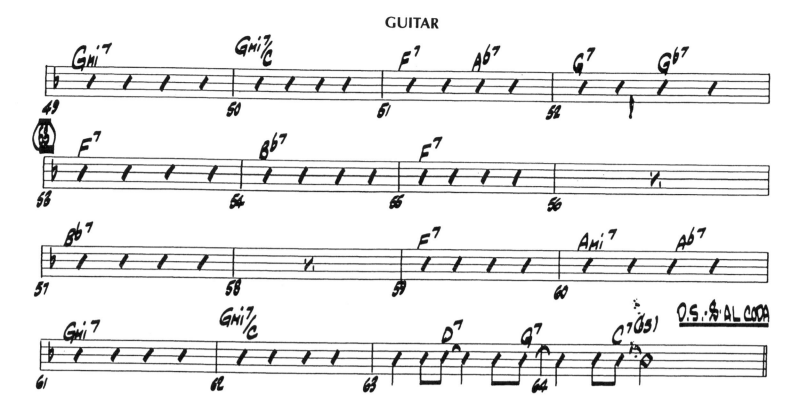

# ST. LOUIS BLUES

**Words and Music by W.C. HANDY**
*Arranged by MICHAEL SWEENEY*

GUITAR

**GUITAR**

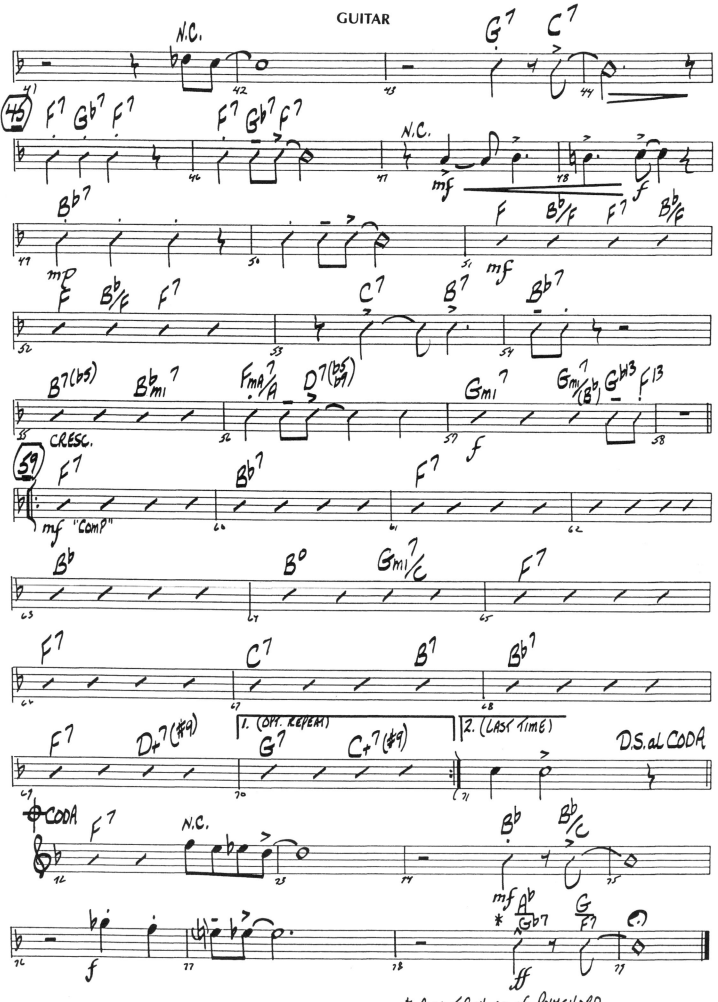

* PLAY TOP CHORD OF POLYCHORD

# WHEN I FALL IN LOVE

Words by EDWARD HEYMAN
Music by VICTOR YOUNG
Arranged by ROGER HOLMES

Guitar

GUITAR

F/C Gmi7/C FMA7/C
Gmi7 C7(b9)
DbMA7 GbMA9
Bbmi7
41
AbMA7 F7(no5)
Bbmi7 Bbmi7/Eb
Ab6 F+7
Bbmi7 Eb7(b9)
f mp
Ab6
Gb9 F7(no5)
Bbmi7
Bbmi7/Eb Eb7(b9)
49
AbMA7 Abo7
Bbmi7 Eb7(b9)
AbMA7
Bbmi7
57
mp mf
Gmi7 C7(b9)
F2
Eb9 D7(no5)
Gmi7
BbMA7/C
65
Eb9
F/C Gmi7/C FMA7/C
DbMA7
Ab/Eb Db/Eb Ab/Eb
Dbmi7 Gb9
BbMA9 EbMA9 Ab13/9 FMA9(#11)
Rit. mp